Potty Training Girls

...the easy way

Simone Cave and
Dr Caroline Fertleman

LIBRARIES NI
WITHDRAWN FROM STOCK

Vermilion
LONDON

Published in 2009 by Vermilion, an imprint of Ebury Publishing

Ebury Publishing is a Random House Group company

Copyright © Simone Cave and Dr Caroline Fertleman 2009

Simone Cave and Dr Caroline Fertleman have asserted their right to be identified as the authors of this Work in accordance with the Copyright, Designs and Patents Act 1988.

All rights reserved. No part of this publication may be reproduced, stored in a retrieval system, or transmitted in any form or by any means, electronic, mechanical, photocopying, recording or otherwise, without the prior permission of the copyright owner.

The Random House Group Limited Reg. No. 954009

Addresses for companies within the Random House Group can be found at www.randomhouse.co.uk

A CIP catalogue record for this book is available from the British Library

Penguin Random House is committed to a sustainable future for our business, our readers and our planet. This book is made from Forest Stewardship Council® certified paper.

MIX
Paper from
responsible sources
FSC® C018179

Printed and bound in Great Britain by Clays Ltd, St Ives plc

ISBN 9780091929145

Copies are available at special rates for bulk orders. Contact the sales development team on 020 7840 8487 for more information.

To buy books by your favourite authors and register for offers, visit www.randomhouse.co.uk

The information in this book has been compiled by way of general guidance in relation to the specific subjects addressed, but is not a substitute and not to be relied on for medical, healthcare, pharmaceutical or other professional advice on specific circumstances and in specific locations. Please consult your GP before changing, stopping or starting any medical treatment. So far as the authors are aware the information given is correct and up to date as at May 2009. Practice, laws and regulations all change, and the reader should obtain up-to-date professional advice on any such issues. The authors and publishers disclaim, as far as the law allows, any liability arising directly or indirectly from the use, or misuse, of the information contained in this book.

We dedicate this book to our daughters
Natalie and Betsy.

CONTENTS

CONTENTS

ACKNOWLEDGEMENTS

With thanks to:

Paul Johnson, Judy Cave and Barbara Levy.

Introduction

ittle girls are known to be sensible, mature and generally more advanced than little boys the same age. This is because their brains actually develop earlier than boys'. Boys tend to use just the left-hand side of their brain, which thinks analytically. Girls use both the left-hand side and also the creative right-hand side at the same time because the neural pathway between the left and right side is more efficient. This is why girls generally develop language skills earlier, and this difference continues until the age of five when boys catch up. If this sounds like your daughter, it certainly bodes well for potty training. With a bit of encouragement from you she should leave her nappies behind with a minimum of fuss and puddles.

Unfortunately, things don't always go by the book. Life can get in the way of the most carefully laid plans. It's well known, for instance, that stressful events such as a new sibling or moving house can have a big impact on potty training. Also, although you hear fewer problems about girls learning to use the potty, all children are different; just because your child is female it doesn't guarantee she will be mature and sensible. Plenty of little girls are boisterous, slower to mature and struggle to concentrate.

We've taken all this into account and have written this book to guide you gently through the process of potty training, whatever your situation. Our flexible approach makes the transition from nappies to the toilet smooth, stress-free and fun for all little girls. If you hit a stumbling block, we'll show you step by step how to deal with the problem. By following our potty-training programme your daughter will learn to use the potty in just a couple of weeks – or, if you're particularly lucky, even sooner.

It tends to be Mum who potty trains her daughter, but anyone caring for your little girl can use this book. We've included a special section for dads – it's not always easy for fathers to take their young daughters to the toilet so we've given lots of tips.

WHAT AGE SHOULD SHE BEGIN?

This is the million-dollar question. In the UK, the average age for little girls is around two and a quarter (two and a half for boys). As all children are different your daughter may not be ready to potty train until she is older – sometimes nearer her third birthday than her second. She may, however, be ready from as young as 18 months. There's nothing you can do to change the age at which she develops and becomes ready – this is down to nature. What you *can* do is observe her carefully and spot the signs that she's ready to begin (*see Chapter 1*).

Getting the timing right is key to successful potty training. If you push your daughter too early she'll probably take longer to learn, and may even have to go back into nappies for a few weeks. A US study published in the journal *Pediatrics* found that training before the age of 27 months nearly always takes longer than training a child after this age.

Don't be in too much of a rush – it's not a competition. Your daughter won't turn around in 20 years and thank you for the fact that she was out of nappies three months earlier than her best friend. On the other hand, she may well have something to say about the fact that you pushed her into using the potty too soon and she ended up getting stressed and frustrated, still wetting herself at the age of five.

Be patient, wait until your daughter is ready, and the process will be swift with no tears.

OUR METHOD

Our method consists of having potty-training 'sessions', beginning with just an hour a day without a nappy and gradually building up until your daughter never wears a nappy at home during the day. The next stage is to leave the house without a nappy (*see Chapter* 6).

It's a very gentle approach that can be fitted around a busy schedule, even if you work full time or have other children. You don't have to do a 'session' every day – our method will work if you just manage weekends and perhaps a couple of sessions during the week at bath time. Unlike more intensive methods which take an all-or-nothing approach, there's no need to take a week off work and cancel social engagements while you spend time locked indoors with your daughter mopping up accidents. Our much more laid-back approach allows potty training to fit around your family and situation.

FRONT BOTTOM, URETHRA OR WEE-WEE HOLE?

Choosing a 'name' for girls' bits is never easy. You'll need to think of something by the time your daughter is about one because this is the age she'll probably start playing with herself on the changing table. There's no need to stop her doing this because it's entirely normal – it's natural, inquisitive behaviour. She is just exploring in the same way that she may also have discovered and played with her toes, hair or belly button. It's a good opportunity to begin teaching her the name of her different body parts.

While urethra is the anatomically correct name for the opening from which urine comes, most little girls won't like this term. Another downside of getting too technical is that you could find yourself having to refer to the vagina, labia and perineum. This would result in a lot of complicated names for a young child to learn, and even if she manages, chances are few other people will understand what she's talking about – particularly her peers.

Try to think of something easy to understand that your daughter will be comfortable saying at school. It's also got to be appropriate to say in front of your GP, as well as other family members. We've found that 'wee hole' is a good choice – it's an accurate description and yet sounds suitably childish. You can then also refer to 'poo hole' and, when it arises, 'baby hole'.

Other choices that work include front and back passage – again simple but accurate descriptions. The good old-fashioned 'front bottom' is still remarkably popular, as is 'fanny', although this is considered a bit rude by some. If you're travelling to the US, it's worth remembering that Americans use 'fanny' as a slang word for the bottom. There are all sorts of other nicknames, including 'twinkle' and 'minkie', which are fine to use if this is what your family is comfortable with. However, do give your daughter an alternative name for when she starts nursery and school so that she won't risk being teased.

You may also decide to call urine and faeces 'wee' and 'poo' – as we have done in this book. Everyone understands these terms including teachers, doctors and children.

1

Is She Ready?

1

Is She Ready?

If you try to coax your daughter out of nappies before she's ready you may run into problems. As we've said before, the average age for little girls to come out of nappies is about two and a quarter, but how do you know if your daughter is going to be one of the early ones or if she needs to wait a bit longer? Well, there are lots of signs to watch out for which indicate she is both physically and mentally ready (*see below*). If you monitor your daughter closely and get the timing right, you'll find that potty training only takes a couple of weeks with very few accidents.

Although it's known that girls are easier to train than boys, the downside of this is that it puts more pressure on them to come out of nappies earlier. So it's particularly important with girls to ignore competitive friends and family who tell you when they think your daughter should start using the potty. The very best person to decide when the time is right is you.

Even your daughter may be keen to come out of nappies before she's physically ready. However enthusiastic she is about using a potty, if she's not physically developed enough to be able to know when she needs a wee or poo then she's going to have accidents. This can be particularly upsetting for little girls because most are keen to get things right and to please their parents. You'll have to persuade her to wait a couple of months without dampening her enthusiasm. Explain to her that her bladder ('the bag in her tummy where her wee is stored') isn't yet strong enough but it will be very soon, and when it is she can have a go at using the potty. If your daughter is reluctant to take no for an answer then you could also try pull-up nappies. You can call them 'big girl knicker nappies' and let your daughter help pull them on.

CHECKLIST

Signs that She's Physically Ready

☐ **She is able to walk and is stable on her feet.** This is because learning to walk requires intense concentration as your daughter discovers how to use her voluntary muscles. It's too much to expect her to be consistently aware of her bodily functions as well (needing to wee and poo). It would simply overload her system if she had to learn to use the potty at the same time as learning to walk.

☐ **Her bowel muscles are fully developed.** From as young as eight months you'll notice that your little girl starts pooing at around the same time each day and poos less frequently than when she was a tiny baby. This is because her bowel muscles are developing. By the time she is two, she'll probably be going once or twice a day. But still go ahead with potty training even if your daughter doesn't quite fit this pattern because everybody's different when it comes to bowel movements.

☐ **Her bladder muscles are fully developed.** Bladder muscles mature later than the bowel, usually between 20 months and two years. You'll notice that your daughter has fewer wet nappies until eventually she can go for about three hours or longer without weeing. This is because the urethral sphincter muscles become more developed – these are the muscles that hold urine in the bladder, and as they strengthen your daughter will develop bladder control.

☐ **She's aware that she's doing a wee or a poo.** Between the ages of 18 months and two years, your little girl will develop awareness that she's going to the toilet. This generally happens a few months earlier with girls than with boys. Your daughter may start telling you that she's doing a wee or a poo, or perhaps she'll stop playing and squat. She may also tell you when her nappy is wet or soiled.

Signs that She's Mentally Ready

☐ **She's happy to have a go at sitting on a potty.** Children need to be mature enough to actually want to use the potty or toilet before you can start training them.

☐ **She's interested in other people going to the toilet.** Girls tend to show interest several months earlier than boys, which is one of the reasons they tend to come out of nappies sooner.

☐ **She can talk.** As well as being mentally mature enough to begin potty training, your daughter also needs adequate language development so that you can talk to each other about if and when she needs the toilet; and she'll need to understand your instructions and all the praise when she succeeds. As we've already mentioned, language is another area where girls are ahead of boys.

GETTING THE TIMING RIGHT

Timing is important when it comes to potty training. In an ideal world we would all pick a time when we're just following our normal routines because this is when stress levels tend to be lowest. If you've got a big event looming, such as a new baby or moving house, then ideally you should postpone potty training until afterwards.

With girls you can sometimes make exceptions. This is because girls tend to find potty training less stressful than boys. Indeed, some little girls learn to use the potty so quickly that it's easy enough to get them trained before big life events. It can be very convenient to get your little girl out of nappies before, say, a new baby arrives.

Wait a Few Months if...

- Your daughter has ever shown reluctance about sitting on a potty or been worried about the toilet flushing. This shows that she is likely to find potty training quite stressful. Coupled with the stress of a big event, it could all get a bit much for her.
- Your daughter is anxious about an up-and-coming event – for example, she knows you're moving house and seems to be having more tantrums.
- You feel you've got enough to cope with for the moment and having to deal with potty training as well would be just too much stress.

Go for It if...

- She can walk, talk (or at least say enough single words to make herself understood), is aware of doing a wee or poo and is enthusiastic about potties. If she's showing all the physical and mental signs listed above and is eager to give it a try then she'll probably learn very quickly.
- She's not having many tantrums or playing up. This indicates that she's happy and not anxious about anything.
- She's able to concentrate and doesn't lose patience with what she's doing. For example, she will calmly spend time doing puzzles even if she finds them difficult. This shows that she enjoys learning so is unlikely to find potty training too frustrating when she has accidents.

If you decide to 'go for it', do be prepared to abandon potty training after a couple of days if it turns out that your daughter isn't ready. This is particularly important if you're attempting to squeeze it in before a big event as stress levels will be higher. So if your daughter doesn't seem to be picking it up quickly, gets confused about when she's about to wee or poo and doesn't ask for the potty, then you'll have to face the fact that she probably isn't ready.

Don't make too much of stopping potty training. Simply say something like, 'That was fun, wasn't it? Perhaps we'll have another go after the baby is born.' Even if she's not yet ready, there's still plenty you can teach her so that when she does finally come out of nappies the process is as seamless as possible. In the next chapter, we explain how to help your daughter prepare to begin potty training.

Training in Time for Nursery

If your daughter is going to start pre-school nursery at the age of three, she'll be expected to be potty trained. Although most little girls are trained long before their third birthday, if your daughter is slower to mature then you'll feel pressurised by this nursery 'deadline' to get her out of nappies.

Try not to pass this pressure on to your daughter because it will delay things further. Call the nursery and explain what stage she is at with toilet training and they will probably put your mind at rest. They are so used to accidents that they will even have a box of spare clothes.

If they don't sound very understanding, then we advise postponing your daughter's nursery place for a term or even choosing a different, more understanding nursery (it's often possible to get a place at the last minute because other parents may change their plans and pull out). A few months won't make any difference in the long term. It's important that she doesn't get upset by unsympathetic teachers if she has lots of accidents. Once the pressure is off, you'll feel a lot more relaxed. Your daughter will pick up on this and will probably learn to use the toilet very quickly.

Do bear in mind that boys tend to have more accidents at nursery than girls, so the teachers won't be expecting your daughter to need constant reminding about the toilet or to have frequent accidents. It's important to mention to them if she needs a bit of help.

It's also common for children to regress in the weeks leading up to the start of term because they feel a bit anxious about going to nursery. Don't worry too much if your daughter is suddenly having lots of accidents; there's every chance that once she starts nursery she'll quickly improve.

Our final tip is to take her to the toilet when you arrive at the nursery, especially if she's not yet accident-free. She'll enjoy the child-sized toilets and low sinks used in nurseries and will soon get used to them. If she's at nursery for only a few hours, the chances are she won't need the toilet again until you pick her up. Don't worry if she does wet herself at nursery (or even soil her pants). Most children have accidents, particularly during their first term, so the staff will be geared up for it.

2

Early Preparation for Potty Training

From around the age of one, your daughter will start to watch and learn what happens when you go to the loo. So, even if your little girl isn't yet ready to begin potty training (*see Chapter 1*), there's plenty you can do to help her in the meantime. Follow our tips and by the time you take your daughter out of nappies she'll not only be familiar and comfortable with bodily functions, but will be able to understand how to use the toilet too.

TIPS FOR PREPARING FOR POTTY TRAINING

Take her to the Loo with You

You probably already take your little girl to the toilet sometimes because it's more convenient than leaving her outside. Don't stop as your daughter gets older because the more familiar she is with the toilet, the quicker she'll learn to use it herself when the time is right, and the less likely she is to be afraid. You'll find that sometimes she will be more interested in playing with the toilet paper than watching you, but at other times she'll be fascinated by what you're doing. Don't be embarrassed; she's just curious in the same innocent way that she's curious if you put on mascara or make a phone call. Chat away about what you're doing and make sure that you wipe from front to back because your daughter will eventually imitate you.

When you wash your hands, encourage your daughter to do the same. This will instil good habits and make the whole process of going to the toilet into a fun game. You can also let her climb on to the toilet at home (when the seat is down) and flush it. Make this a bit of a treat, saying, 'You're such a big girl, would you like to flush the toilet?' This will increase her confidence and reduce the chances of her ever becoming frightened of sitting on the loo, or being 'sucked away' down a flushing toilet.

Public Toilets

When you're out with your daughter and need the loo, the easiest way to take her into a public toilet with you is to choose a disabled toilet and wheel her buggy in. This isn't always an option, however, so you may need to hold her in one arm and go to the loo one-handed – not easy but just about possible if you're desperate.

Once your daughter can walk and is too heavy to hold, she'll be busy playing with the lock on the door and the sanitary bin while you go to the loo. Try not to get cross because it's important that your daughter doesn't associate toilets with being told off. Instead you could give your daughter a 'job' such as holding your handbag, and if she still insists on squeezing round the back of the toilet and touching the seat, make sure that you wash her hands thoroughly afterwards.

It's important that you wipe the seat of public toilets and sit down, rather than squat. Again, your daughter will be watching closely and will imitate you when she's old enough, and she won't be able to squat over a toilet because she'll be too short.

Show Your Daughter her Dirty Nappy

From time to time, show your little girl her dirty nappy and chat about how you're putting on a fresh nappy and cleaning the poo off her bottom. Let her feel the heavy weight of a wet nappy and explain that it is heavier than a dry nappy because she's done lots of wee. This will give your daughter the message that going to the toilet is a natural process and nothing to be ashamed of. It's important to convey this, so don't ever show feelings of revulsion if you're changing a particularly smelly or leaky nappy.

Don't Get Angry if Your Little Girl 'Plays with Poo'

If you've ever walked into your little girl's nursery and discovered that she's taken off her nappy and smeared poo over her cot, herself and the walls, your natural reaction will have been horror, shock and revulsion. Surely little girls just don't do this sort of thing? Well, unfortunately some do (and boys too) but it doesn't mean that she's got behavioural problems, and she's certainly not being naughty. She's just being curious. Plenty of children do this – some even taste their poo!

It's important that you remain calm while you clean up, however much you want to yell and scream, because your daughter will be confused if you're angry about her poo. Getting very cross can occasionally lead to 'withholding constipation' (*see Chapter 9*), a condition that can affect toddlers if their carers have shown revulsion about their nappies and poos.

If your daughter repeatedly removes her nappy, put her sleep suit on back-to-front so that she can't reach the poppers.

Ensure that Carers are Comfortable Changing Your Daughter's Nappy

Scientists have shown that mums object to the smell of their own baby's poo less than that of other people's babies. In a study published in the *Journal of Evolution and Human Behaviour* (July 2006), mums were given 'anonymous' nappies to smell, and they found the smell of their own baby's nappy 'less revolting' than those of other babies.

It's thought that the 'disgust instinct' is overridden in mums to encourage them to nurture their babies – they would be less likely to do so if they found them repellent. This research demonstrates that carers may genuinely find changing your daughter's nappy more disgusting than you do. So be aware of this and ensure that people caring for your baby don't have any hang-ups that your daughter could pick up on.

Use Bath Time for Practice

Keep a potty in the bathroom from the time your daughter is about 15 months old so that she can play with it before her bath when she's naked. Tell her what the potty is for and that she can sit on it if she wants to. Your daughter may also like to sit on the potty fully clothed and imitate you when you go to the loo, so keep the potty near your toilet.

She's almost certainly too young to actually use her potty, but it's good to have one around so that she's familiar with it. Don't worry if she's not interested. You've got months before you will potty train her and there's no need to get stressed in the meantime. Let her become curious in her own time and don't try and force it. If she does happen to sit on it, then do give her lots of praise.

Your daughter is bound to wee in the bath but you usually won't notice because she'll be sitting. Never try and stop her because it would give negative messages. From 12 months onwards she may stand up more in the bath, especially if you use a non-slip bath mat. If you happen to notice her weeing, point it out, saying, 'You're doing a wee, what a clever girl.' This will help your daughter to become aware of when she's weeing, and awareness is the first step to control.

Make Use of her Dolls

Dolls can be useful throughout the toilet-training programme. Girls have an advantage over boys in that most of them love dolls. You can buy dolls that wee and have potties, which can be helpful in encouraging your daughter to understand the potty-training process. Any doll can help her learn, however, because you can encourage her to sit it on the potty that you keep in the bathroom. It's a known teaching technique to allow the pupil to teach someone else the skill they are trying to acquire.

Helping your daughter to be aware of potties, toilets and bodily functions will give her a big advantage when she starts to actually use the potty. She will already have a pretty good idea about the 'theory' of potty training and all she'll have to do is put it into practice.

3

Countdown to the Big Day

When your daughter is showing signs that she is both physically and mentally ready to begin potty training and you know that D-day is imminent (*see Chapter 1*), there are several steps to take. You must prepare your daughter for what's about to happen; prepare your home; and finally take your daughter on a shopping spree to buy the kit such as knickers and stickers. Here's our guide to gearing up for the big day.

PREPARE YOUR DAUGHTER

When you're both feeling relaxed, tell your daughter that you think she's ready to stop wearing nappies quite soon. If you have followed our tips in Chapter 2 she'll have a reasonable understanding of potties and what they are for, and there's a good chance that she will be keen to try using one.

Talk her through the process and *ask* her if she'd like to give potty training a go. Explain that you'll have to go to the shops together to choose potties and knickers. She'll probably be very enthusiastic, but if she's not ready and seems reluctant, that's fine. Tell her that she can wait a few more weeks if she wants to. Some little girls need a bit longer to get their heads around starting something new, and it's much better to let them be ready in their own time than to push.

Once she has agreed to give potty training a try then tell her when the shopping trip will be, and also talk her through what will happen when she has an accident. Explain that she may accidentally wee or poo on the floor or in her new knickers from time to time while she's learning. Emphasise that this is okay because you'll clean it up with wipes and so on, and put the soiled knickers in the washing machine then give her some nice clean ones to wear. It really helps little girls to understand the process of accidents and cleaning up before the event because they can become quite upset if they make a mess or 'spoil' their new knickers.

PREPARE YOUR HOME

Choose the room in which you want to begin potty training. If you have a room with old carpets or a floor that's easy to clean, this may be an obvious choice. Make sure the 'training room' is warm enough – you may need to turn up the heating by a couple of degrees during the winter months because your daughter will be semi-naked in the early stages of potty training.

You can use plastic-backed bathmats to protect your floor and sofa, with your daughter sitting on the soft side. If you don't want to risk your carpet getting soiled you can always set up a play area in the corner of the kitchen, if it's big enough. Using the garden is another good option if it's warm enough to play outside. Lots of mums wait until the summer to get their toddlers out of nappies – as well as sparing your carpets, there's less washing because children wear fewer clothes in the warmer months. However, there's no need to be limited to the summer because when your daughter is ready to begin, she'll learn to use the potty and toilet very quickly and there shouldn't be many accidents.

GO SHOPPING

Once your little girl has given you the go-ahead that she wants to start using the potty, you can go shopping together for knickers and toilet-training equipment. Talk to her about this shopping trip in advance so that she can look forward to it and have a few days to think about and get used to the idea of coming out of nappies. By the time you hit the shops she'll be very enthusiastic and will love choosing pretty knickers and fancy star charts.

Shopping List

Here are some useful potty-training gadgets worth buying. Let your daughter make some of the choices, although she obviously doesn't have to be present for every purchase.

Two Identical Cheap Plastic Potties

We strongly advise getting two identical potties because you can keep one in the play area and one in the bathroom and you'll avoid a situation where your daughter refuses point blank to use the 'red' potty. If you've already got a potty in the bathroom that's fine because there's no harm in having spare potties that you can keep around your home.

Cheap plastic potties are ideal because they're small and easy to clean. Also, your daughter will squat right down on the floor with her feet on the ground – this is a better position for pooing than sitting on a larger-style potty. Don't worry about potties having splashguards on them; these are to stop boys making too much mess but won't affect your daughter in any way. She can sit with the splashguard at the front or the back, whichever she chooses. Your little girl should definitely be involved in choosing her potty, but you'll have to steer her away from the larger, fancy potties. She'll still enjoy selecting the colour.

Knickers

Do let her have her say in what she wants. She may opt for something pretty and girly, or choose her favourite television character like Dora the Explorer. We've found that if she likes her knickers she'll not only be keener to wear them, but also to keep them dry. If she can't make up her mind then buy a couple of packs – they'll get plenty of use, especially if you buy knickers in a size bigger than her age (we recommend doing this as it makes it much easier to pull them up and down).

Big Leggings and Tights

Most children don't have the manual dexterity to cope with buttons and complicated clothes until they are about four. So stock up on leggings (not too tight) as these are easy to pull up and down, enabling your daughter to go to the toilet alone when the time comes. Tights in a larger size than she normally wears are also helpful – these will be easier for you to yank down quickly and also easier for your daughter to manage by herself as she progresses. Elasticised trousers also work, and jogging-style bottoms are a very practical, albeit unfeminine, option.

Pretty Stickers

Little girls love stickers so hunt out some that she hasn't had before and thinks are a bit special. A reward chart helps spur on most girls – you can buy a ready-made chart from large supermarkets and stationers. Alternatively, make your own using a thick piece of A4 paper or card. Write a list of training achievements down one side, such as sitting on the potty; doing a wee in the potty; doing a poo in the potty; pulling down knickers; pulling up knickers; washing hands. You can draw simple pictures for each of these activities then draw horizontal lines across the card so that each activity has its own space for stars and stickers. Every time your little girl completes an activity, she gets a star or sticker – you can buy these, or just draw on stars.

A Mini Toilet Seat

Children can find sitting on the loo quite frightening because it's high up and large enough for them to fall down. So it's important to get your daughter a child's toilet seat that scales down the toilet to her size. We particularly recommend those with side handles as these give your daughter something to hold on to.

A Stepping Stool

This will help your daughter climb on to the toilet, and then she can rest her feet on it for added security. She can also use it to reach the sink to wash her hands. You can buy cheap plastic stools designed for this purpose.

A Folding Toilet Seat

This can be helpful when you're out and about because your daughter will feel more secure sitting on a 'smaller' toilet. It will also be more hygienic for her, although you will have to wipe the public toilet seat first so that you don't get your portable seat too dirty. You can buy padded travel seats. Plastic ones are less comfortable but fold smaller.

A Travel Potty

These are particularly useful in the early stages of potty training when your daughter won't have the physical capacity to hold on for more than a minute or two before she wees. The folding potty frame can be whipped out, the legs unfolded, and then you put a bag over the top with a liner at the bottom – or you can put the bag and liner on before you leave home to save time. Once your daughter has been to the toilet you simply throw the bag away. You can also get portable potties with lids. We don't recommend these, however, as they are bulkier and you probably won't want to carry around your daughter's wee and poo.

Try to begin potty training within a few days of your shopping spree while your little girl is enthusiastic. Help her to put her new knickers away, and to put her new potties in place ready to begin. She can start using her stepping stool to wash her hands straight away. Do let her play with her 'new toys' if she wants to.

Don't Waste Your Money on the Following

Fancy Potties

Don't fork out on themed potties including musical ones or those shaped like animals. If your daughter needs this sort of persuasion to sit on the potty she's simply not ready to come out of nappies. Also, it's important that her potty isn't so appealing that she won't switch to the toilet – we encourage her to start using the toilet within the first couple of weeks of our training programme.

Imitation Toilet Potties

Avoid these cumbersome toilet lookalikes, which are large and have lids. They may be more comfortable and appealing to some children, but as we said above, our programme moves from the potty to the real toilet within a couple of weeks so it's not worth spending lots of money on these big potties. They can also be more difficult to clean than a small plastic potty.

Training Pants

These absorbent cloth pants look and feel like real knickers, but they will make your daughter feel wetter than if she was wearing a nappy. The idea is that your daughter will become more aware of when she is weeing and pooing. We think they're a waste of time because when your daughter is truly ready to begin toilet training she'll know when she's weeing and pooing in her nappy anyway. Training pants tend to be used before children are really ready to come out of nappies. It's harder to clean up soiled training pants than a soiled nappy, which you can simply throw away.

Pull-ups

Pull-up nappies are marketed as the most grown-up style of nappy for toddlers. We think that they're a bit of a gimmick and tend to be more expensive. That said, we sometimes recommend them for night-time (when your daughter still needs a nappy at night but feels too grown up to wear one), and also for the occasions when your daughter is insisting on being a big girl and wearing her knickers but you want her to wear a nappy, such as when you're travelling in a car, train or plane.

Don't Try and Take Shortcuts

You may have heard of children who skip the potty stage and instead go directly from nappies to using the toilet. Okay, this avoids having to clean poo-filled potties, and cuts out a step in the potty-training process, but we think it's better to use a potty. In our programme your little girl will move pretty swiftly from a potty to the toilet, but the advantage of getting her on a potty initially is that it puts her in a squatting position which helps pooing. Also, she will be more likely to sit for longer on a potty, which increases her chances of success. Another advantage is that you won't need to stand over and hold her to help her balance as you would with a toilet.

The only exception we make is if your daughter is big for her age, in which case the potty will be very uncomfortable (*see Chapter 5*).

We recommend keeping the potty-training process as simple as possible and just buying what you need to make it a bit more convenient. So although there's a lot of paraphernalia out there, there's no need to get carried away when you shop.

4

D-day

So the day has arrived when the nappy comes off and the puddles begin. This can be a bit daunting for both parents and children. This is why our training method has potty-training 'sessions' that last for only about an hour. So there's no need to cancel your social life or take time off work.

It's all very simple. During a session, your daughter goes without her nappy at home then at the end of the session you put it back on again. The method has been devised to cut the stress of potty training to an absolute minimum. This is important because your little girl shouldn't pick up on any stress and should never feel that by having accidents she is disappointing you. She will progress a lot more quickly if the process is kept very positive.

Some little girls will learn to use the potty in a few days using our method. By all means watch your daughter closely and, if she seems able, you can extend the length and number of potty-training sessions quite quickly. However, it's more likely to take a couple of weeks to get the hang of things.

We suggest that you hold back from taking your daughter out without her nappy on for a couple of weeks after she's got the hang of using the potty and toilet at home. It's obviously more challenging to find a public toilet for girls than boys (who can wee down drains or in the gutter). Girls can be particularly sensitive to having accidents and often feel more self-conscious than boys, so rather than put your daughter through any unnecessary stress we advise waiting a little longer before going out in public without a nappy.

Plenty of little girls have had success using a more intense potty-training method – the all-or-nothing approach where they stop wearing a nappy and that's it. There's no switching from pants to nappies, even when you leave the house. You just go for it and hope for the best. Some experts argue that it's confusing to keep swapping from pants to nappies, but we haven't found this. After all, children seem to cope with wearing a nappy at night and pants during the day.

Using our potty-training sessions approach, you will probably have your daughter out of nappies within a few weeks. Within a few months there's a good chance that you won't even bother to pack spare knickers when you go out.

BEFORE YOU BEGIN

Choose a Time

Pick a morning when you and your daughter are feeling happy and relaxed then suggest, 'Shall we have a go at using the potty today?' A good time to ask is when you're changing your daughter's nappy when she wakes in the morning or after her nap. She should be feeling refreshed and happy at these times.

There's a good chance that she'll feel a bit anxious and say no, in which case leave it for a day or so. This isn't a race and it's important that your little girl doesn't feel pushed into potty training. You can always ask again at bath time when your daughter won't be wearing her nappy.

It doesn't matter what time of day you pick to have a potty-training session, although we suggest that you avoid choosing a time because she's due to have a poo. If your daughter poos at roughly the same time each day it can be tempting to time a potty-training session around this. However, there will be too much anticipation and she'll sense the pressure. The key to our method is to stay relaxed.

Get her Ready

When your daughter says yes, and so gives her 'permission' to begin, help her to choose her knickers and to put them on. Try to avoid tights and trousers because these will make getting to the potty on time more difficult. Also, your little girl will feel more 'bundled up' so will be more likely to forget that she isn't wearing a nappy. You can put on a pair of socks to keep her warm.

Once she's dressed in her knickers, show her where the potty is and put her star chart up. You can also give her a drink – she'll need to wee about 20 minutes after drinking it.

DURING THE SESSION

Sitting on the Potty

At the start of the session, suggest that your daughter has a go at sitting on the potty and explain that she has to pull her knickers down. Chances are she won't need to go the first time, but give her lots of praise anyway. Tell her she's a clever girl just for sitting.

Don't make her sit on the potty for too long – 30 seconds is enough or she'll become uncomfortable and bored. Some training methods suggest sitting a child on the potty in front of a DVD, but we don't recommend this. Our method is about helping the child herself to become aware that she needs to go, rather than randomly catching her wees and poos because she spends so long sitting on the potty.

Wait

Once your daughter has had a go at sitting on her potty, there's little to do apart from wait and see if she happens to need a wee or poo in the next hour or so. In the meantime, play together and keep an eye out for signs that your little girl needs a wee – she may hold herself or wriggle from side to side. Some little girls will want to hide away if they need a poo, or will stop playing and look a bit worried.

If you suspect that she needs to go then suggest that she sits on the potty again. Try not to ask her to sit on the potty more than once every 30 minutes because she'll find it irritating. After all, she's having one-to-one playtime with Mummy so won't want this interrupted too often.

Stars

Ensure that your daughter gets at least one sticker per potty-training session – even for putting her knickers on or sitting on her potty. This will help her associate potty training with success. It's important not to make her feel like a failure, even if she doesn't pick it up quickly.

Her First Accident

If her first wee or poo is on the floor, don't allow her to feel like a failure. Say, 'Ooh, you've done a wee and it's made a puddle on the floor because you're not wearing a ...' and let her fill in the word 'nappy'. Say, 'You're such a big girl that next time you can wee in the potty,' and so on.

If she has a wee accident, wipe her then change her knickers into 'nice fresh ones', then you can clean up the floor together. Be pleasant, but don't give praise or she'll get confused about where she's supposed to wee.

If she has a poo accident, clean her up with wipes as you would after a dirty nappy. Then dress her in clean knickers and put her soiled ones in a nappy bag to be dealt with later. Clean up the poo as quickly and with as little fuss as possible. Stay positive throughout – say, 'Ooh look, the poo has gone in your knickers because you weren't wearing a nappy and next time you can do a poo in the ...' and let her fill in the word potty.

Her First Success

The first time your daughter does a wee or poo in the potty, go crazy with the praise. Clap, kiss her, phone Daddy to tell him and award her a particularly pretty sticker. Give her your full attention and loads of praise for at least a few minutes, and she'll soon be on that potty again. The idea is that she gets far more attention for a success than an accident.

Wiping

Explain that when she's wearing pants she has to wipe herself after using the potty. Then, when she does a wee or poo, wipe her from front to back 'just like Mummy'. Don't let her wipe herself just yet because this needs to be done carefully, particularly after a poo, to avoid her getting the bacterial infection vulvovaginitis (*see Chapter 9*). This is when bacteria are transferred from the anal region to the vagina and vulva.

Let your daughter become used to you wiping her over the next couple of days because she's going to need your help with wiping after a poo until she is about five or six, when she'll be able to competently wipe herself. And you'll need to help her wipe after a wee until she is about three when she'll have the manual dexterity to wipe herself.

You may need to teach your daughter to wipe herself after a poo when she starts nursery at three – she won't be very competent but on the few occasions when she's on her own, at least she'll be able to have a go.

If your daughter is fiercely independent and wants to do it herself, suggest that she tears the paper off the roll so that she feels involved – she'll find this quite difficult.

Over the coming days and weeks as your daughter learns to wee in her potty reliably, she can have a go at wiping after a wee. Show her how to hold the paper and wipe from front to back. A dabbing rather than a rubbing action is less likely to result in spreading bacteria.

AFTER THE SESSION

Nappy Back On

As soon as you put your daughter's nappy back on, there's a good chance that she'll do a wee or poo. This can seem quite irritating as you ask yourself why she couldn't have done this in the potty. However, it's actually a good sign and indicates that she has some control – she was simply feeling too anxious during the session to wee or poo and waited until she was securely back in her nappy again. This will change as your daughter gains confidence over the next few sessions. She will probably do a wee or poo in the potty within a couple of days because she is obviously aware enough to be able to hang on. All you can do is stay relaxed about where she wees or poos as this will take any pressure off and help her feel in control.

Cleaning Up

If your daughter managed to wee or poo in her potty then tip the contents down the loo and wipe the potty with antibacterial wipes. For a more thorough clean, you can also use an antibacterial spray, but do make sure you rinse this off carefully. To clean soiled knickers, use a wipe to scrape the worst of the poo into the toilet, then rinse the knickers in a bucket before putting them in the washing machine.

Check the Star Chart

Count how many stickers or stars your daughter has earned today. Praise her even if it's just one. Tell her that she can show Daddy when he comes home, and talk about how she can earn even more stars next time – by doing a wee in the potty perhaps.

Should You Proceed?

After your little girl's first potty-training session, you may feel that she simply isn't ready to come out of nappies yet. The following will help you decide whether to continue (in which case turn to Chapter 5), or whether to postpone potty training for a few weeks. If you decide to postpone it, simply don't mention potty training to your daughter for a little while – there's no need to make a big deal about it.

She Wouldn't Put her Knickers on

Don't insist that your little girl wears her knickers if she seems to be objecting. This may be her way of telling you that she's not ready to come out of nappies. Before you postpone potty training, try the following:

- Try her with nothing on her bottom half – it may take your daughter a week or so to come round to the idea of wearing pants.
- Buy some plainer knickers – sometimes little girls are worried about weeing or pooing in their very pretty knickers. Don't worry about wasting money on lots of different knickers – they'll get plenty of use over the coming months.

She Refused to Sit on her Potty

Again, this may be your daughter's way of saying she wants to stay in nappies for a bit longer. Before you postpone potty training, try asking if she'd like to sit on a different potty. If her potty in the bathroom is pink with stickers on it, and it's the one she's used to playing with, then she may want to sit on this one rather than the plainer potty you've given her for her potty session. Try swapping the potties and you may have an instant solution to the problem. (This is why we advised buying two identical potties in Chapter 3.)

She Has Accidents

Of course children will have accidents during their early potty-training sessions, but you have to work out why. If your daughter was too busy playing to notice that she needed the toilet then continue with the sessions. If, however, she has no idea about when she's about to poo or wee and seemed frustrated or bored during the session, this suggests that she is still too immature to come out of nappies.

Before you postpone potty training, try the following:

- Think back over the last few weeks and see if you can remember your daughter ever announcing that she needed a wee or poo. This is a good indicator of whether or not she is mature enough for potty training.

- Try having a potty-training session at a different time of day – perhaps when your little girl is less tired or hungry as these factors can make children irritable and unable to concentrate and learn.

In an ideal world, everyone who reads this book will sail through D-day and proceed to the next stage of our potty-training programme. We don't expect that to happen, though, and realise that plenty of little girls won't be ready yet. If your daughter is one of these, try to stay relaxed because it really makes no difference in the long term whether she learns to use a potty quickly or slowly.

5

The Next Two
Weeks

I f D-day went well and your daughter seemed to enjoy her potty-training session then here's how to progress. Have as many or as few sessions in a day as you like – just do what fits around your schedule and family. Keeping things relaxed in this way will accelerate your daughter's learning. Don't be tempted to cram in too many sessions to try to push your daughter along because this will take the fun out of it. We suggest a maximum of three sessions a day for the first week, gradually extending the time that the nappy stays off. Don't worry if you happen to miss a day or two. It really doesn't matter; you can just carry on where you left off. The beauty of this training programme is that it is very flexible.

The following timetable is a rough estimate. All little girls are different and your daughter may progress faster or slower. It's not a race and it really doesn't matter whether it takes your daughter two days or over two months to get the hang of potty training. The important thing is that it remains fun and that you follow your daughter's lead. So only move on to the next stage when you're sure she's ready, not when you think she should be ready.

DAYS TWO AND THREE

Continue with the potty sessions, reminding your daughter to sit on the potty every 30 minutes or so. Give her lots of praise and stickers. If things seem to be going well and your little girl is enjoying the sessions, feel free to fit in up to three sessions a day, depending on your schedule. You can also lengthen the sessions to a couple of hours or more without a nappy – this will increase the chances of your little girl actually needing to go to the toilet during a session.

What You Can Expect

The first few sessions will result in accidents and the occasional wee or poo in the potty – usually after you've reminded your daughter to go. You'll notice that she soon becomes more confident about sitting on her potty and wees in it more frequently, perhaps even doing a poo.

What you're ultimately hoping for is that she will

actually tell you that she needs to do a wee or poo. This is a big milestone because it shows awareness of her bladder or bowel, plus the ability to hold on just about long enough to get to the potty (she'll only be able to hold for a few seconds at first but this will increase over the next few weeks as she matures). She may only ask for the potty once or twice during the early sessions, but this will increase with time.

How You Can Help

When your daughter asks for the potty, make a tremendous fuss, perhaps rewarding her with a particularly pretty sticker for her chart. If she's slower to ask for the potty and needs lots of reminding, stay calm. Remember that if she's done it once then she's got the physical capability and her brain is receiving signals that she needs to go, so she is bound to ask for the potty again quite soon.

If she doesn't ask for the potty at all during the first couple of days, don't worry. Just give her longer before moving on to the next stage, and remind yourself that the best way you can help is by allowing her to progress at her own pace. In the meantime continue to give her lots of encouragement, with a sticker every time she sits on the potty, wees or poos in it or washes her hands.

DAYS FOUR TO SEVEN – USING THE TOILET

Once your little girl has hit the big milestone of being able to ask for the potty, you can show her how to sit on the toilet. Note that she still won't be asking for her potty every time she needs a wee or poo, so do keep reminding her (although you won't be reminding her as often now).

What You Can Expect

Most little girls are willing to try sitting on the toilet but may take a couple of days longer to actually do a wee or poo. Eventually, your little girl should be as confident about weeing and pooing in the toilet as she is in her potty. Soon she'll hardly bother with her potty.

How You Can Help

Suggest that your daughter has a go at sitting on the toilet at bath time (she won't be wearing clothes and you'll both be near the loo so no last-minute dashes). If she refuses to sit on the toilet then respect her decision and simply repeat the suggestion in a couple of days. As long as you stay relaxed, she'll soon give it a go.

Give your daughter masses of praise for simply sitting on the toilet, even if she doesn't go – the toilet can seem very big to small children, and the flushing can be a bit scary. When she does finally wee or poo in the toilet give plenty of praise and stickers.

Continue to allow your daughter to wee in the potty if she wants to because she will have come to associate it with getting lots of praise. Be prepared, too, for her to have days when she doesn't feel up to the challenge of using the toilet. Never give your daughter the message that there's anything wrong with using the potty. In fact, travel potties can be invaluable when you're out and about and there are no nearby toilets (*see page 75*).

Garden Practice

If you've got a garden then encourage your little girl to squat down and wee in it because this will be an immense help when you're out. Small children have small bladders so can't hang on long, so if you're not near a toilet you may have to take emergency measures. If your daughter is comfortable with weeing behind a tree this will sometimes save her having an accident. So teach her to wee in the great outdoors – a skill she will occasionally resort to right into adulthood!

WEEK TWO – MORE PRACTICE AT HOME

Continue the sessions and using the toilet at home until your daughter rarely wears a nappy during the day and is able to tell you more than 50 per cent of the time that she needs the toilet. Children still need a bit of reminding for weeks, and sometimes months, after they're 'potty trained'. The aim is to build your daughter's confidence before you venture out so that you can minimise accidents outside the home.

What You Can Expect

Your daughter will soon become more or less toilet trained at home. She may even take herself off to the toilet, although this usually takes a few weeks longer. You can expect her to have the occasional accident for a couple of months. Don't worry – just react as normal in a calm, reassuring way.

How You Can Help

It's essential that you remain relaxed and avoid putting pressure on your daughter. Just give her lots of encouragement and watch her confidence grow.

TROUBLESHOOTING

She Willingly Sits on the Potty but Seems Unable to Wee

Lots of little girls sit on the potty but don't seem able to wee. This is because they aren't yet physically mature enough to know when they need to wee. If this is the case, you need to give your daughter another month or so to mature, so stop the potty sessions for now. Don't make a big deal about stopping the sessions because you don't want your little girl to feel like a failure.

If your daughter is particularly big or tall for her age, she may feel hunched up and uncomfortable on the potty. You could try moving straight to the toilet, but do use a child's toilet seat so that she feels secure.

She Becomes Tearful Every Time She Has an Accident

Some girls hate 'spoiling' their pretty knickers. Explain to her how easy it is to clean her knickers – she can help put the knickers in the washing machine and switch it on. Perhaps she could try not wearing any knickers for a few days while she builds confidence in weeing and pooing in her potty. It's important to give masses of reassurance about accidents and to tell your daughter that even Mummy and Daddy (and any other adults she admires) had accidents when they were little.

She Refuses to Sit on the Toilet

Little girls tend to be quite brave compared with boys, so your daughter will probably be willing to sit on the toilet. If she is hesitant then help to build her confidence by allowing her to flush away the wee and poo from her potty. Once you've tipped it down the loo, 'reward' her by letting her climb on to the closed seat so that she can flush the toilet as a special treat. Without realising, she'll come to associate getting on the toilet as a treat rather than something scary.

It's important not to pressurise her into sitting on the toilet. This has to be done in her own time – all you can do is casually suggest she gives it a try. Ensure that you've got a child's loo seat installed plus a stepping stool as both of these help children cope with the large size of a toilet.

She Won't Put her Nappy on to Go out

If your daughter is reluctant to wear a nappy when you're going out, by all means allow her to go nappy-less if you think she'll probably be okay (*see Chapter 6* for more on coping when you're out and about). Children sometimes know their own capabilities better than their parents. However, if you're pretty sure it will end in tears because she's not ready, persuade your daughter to wear a pull-up nappy – 'grown-up travel knickers'. Pull-ups are also useful for long car journeys, and your daughter can always change into her knickers on arrival. Alternatively, you could use a travel changing mat to protect her car seat – tell your daughter it's a travel mat to make her more comfortable.

If she's adamant that she wants to wear her knickers and refuses even to wear a pull-up, let her have her way. There's nothing to be gained by letting this become a battle. Be especially kind if she has an accident and resist saying 'I told you so', however tempting, as you struggle to clean her up in public.

By the end of this chapter your daughter will no longer wear a nappy at home and will be comfortable about using the potty and toilet. If she needs more time, that's fine. All children are different and it's important that she's happy about leaving her nappy off before you move on to the next stage, which is going out without a nappy on.

6

Out and About

After a couple of weeks you can think about taking your daughter out without her nappy on. Although potty training girls is usually easier than boys, when it comes to going out it can be a bit more challenging because they can't easily wee against the nearest tree or down a drain. It's therefore important to be sure that your daughter is physically capable of 'hanging on' before she wees. You can do this by not rushing to the toilet when you are at home – take your time and see if she is able to wait.

Another tip is to try teaching your daughter to sit on your toilet at home without her child's toilet seat. This can be very useful for using public toilets. Some children (especially those who are tall or agile) will be happy to do this. Whenever your daughter sits on an adult-sized toilet seat, do hold her firmly so that she feels secure and doesn't worry about slipping down the toilet.

If your little girl seems apprehensive about the 'big seat', don't push it – just buy a fold-up children's loo seat (*see Chapter 3*). These fit easily on to public toilet seats to make them smaller and easier for your daughter to sit on. Let your daughter practise with it at home so that it's familiar. It's also worth investing in a travel potty (*see Chapter 3*). Again, let your daughter have a go at using this before venturing out. There's a chance that you'll never have to use it, but it will give peace of mind during those early trips out.

CHECKLIST

The Going-out Checklist

☐ She doesn't wear a nappy at home during the day

☐ She usually tells you when she needs a wee or a poo

☐ She can 'hang on' a couple of minutes before doing a wee or a poo

☐ She is confident about sitting on a toilet (or a fold-up loo seat)

☐ She's happy to use a travel potty

Once you've ticked all of the above, you can take your daughter out and be reasonably confident that she will remain dry. There are bound to be some accidents over the next few weeks so pack spare knickers and tights, wipes and a plastic bag to put soiled clothes into. We also suggest protecting the buggy with a travel changing mat for the first week or so – mainly to minimise your stress and keep things nice and relaxed.

YOUR FIRST TRIPS OUT

Your first outing could be to the supermarket, a local café or a (tolerant) friend's house. Don't go too far from home in the first week – a day trip in the car is obviously more likely to result in accidents.

Tell your daughter where the toilet is when you arrive and ask if she needs to go. Chances are that she won't even go to the toilet on her first few trips out, especially if you keep them short. This stage is about confidence building, so when you get home, do tell your daughter how clever she is to have gone out without her nappy.

It's worth reminding little girls to go to the toilet whenever you happen to be near one. This will reduce the number of tedious public toilet searches. Get into the habit of asking if your daughter needs a wee before you leave home, and whenever you arrive somewhere with a toilet. She may be wary of using an unknown toilet, so tell her you need to go and suggest she comes along too. It's worth finding out where the toilet is in your local supermarket, library or anywhere else you may visit in the early weeks because when your daughter needs a wee you won't have long to get her there.

Public Toilets

Take wipes to wipe the seat, and some tissues in case there's no toilet paper. Also pack antibacterial hand gel in case there's no soap to wash hands afterwards. Some public toilets are particularly dirty, which can be tricky for little girls because they aren't tall enough to 'squat' over the seat. Wipe the seat before lifting her onto it then hold her securely. Your daughter is bound to touch the seat, and perhaps the floor when she bends over to be wiped. Try not to express any disgust as this will make her feel anxious; just use lots of wipes and anti-bacterial hand gel.

You can buy disposable paper toilet-seat covers which work out at about 10 pence each. We don't recommend them, though, because they slip and your daughter may not feel secure sitting on them. It's also important that she doesn't grow up being too fastidious about public toilets – we all need to use them and there's no point being too uptight about them.

Contrary to popular belief, you can't actually 'catch' anything from toilet seats. The only real risk is if your daughter touches the seat, gets some infected poo on her hands and transfers the germs via her mouth, which could give her a tummy bug and diarrhoea. This can be avoided with good hand washing.

Nowhere Near a Toilet

There will be times when your daughter announces she needs a wee or poo and there's just no way that you can get her to a toilet in time. You have a few options:

1. Squat

You may be able to find a quiet spot, perhaps behind a parked car, where you can help her squat. If you're in the country or a park, then she might be able to squat behind a tree. She will probably get wee over her knickers and tights, but don't worry too much – urine is sterile and will soon dry off. Some mums hold their daughters over drains as this is less messy but it's also back-breaking and not recommended.

2. Use the Travel Potty

This is a good option if you've got it with you, especially if your daughter needs a poo.

3. Put a Nappy on

It's worth keeping an emergency nappy in your handbag in the early days because you can put this on your daughter whenever she needs a wee or poo. This is a good solution when you're on public transport with no toilets because a portable potty could spill. Explain that it's just an emergency nappy and that she can take it off again as soon as you are able to clean her up.

Public Accidents

Some little girls are quite self-conscious about wetting themselves, and will be even more distraught if they soil their knickers. Make sure, therefore, that you are organised with a clean-up kit (wipes, nappy bag, clean knickers and tights) so you can sort your daughter out quickly and efficiently, minimising her embarrassment.

Ideally, take her into a baby change area or a disabled toilet where you can stuff her soiled clothes into a plastic bag, clean her up with wipes and give her clean knickers and tights (or trousers). If there's nowhere available, and not even a public toilet nearby, then find a quiet corner and change her out of wet clothes as quickly as possible to avoid fuss and embarrassment. Don't worry about wiping away wee because, as a one-off, being a bit damp won't do her any harm.

If she's soiled her knickers it can be trickier to sort her out, but again try to find a quiet corner and peel off dirty clothes carefully, sealing them in a plastic bag. Use wipes to clean up the worst of the poo – there's no need to do a perfect job in an emergency because you can do a thorough clean-up at home. Just change her into clean clothes.

Never get cross with your daughter for having accidents because she'll find this upsetting. She may even recognise it as a new device to get Mummy's attention, in which case you can expect more public accidents in future. Keep your manner low-key but pleasant: 'Oops, you've done a poo in your knickers. Next time we can find a grown-ups' toilet and you can get a special star.'

Dads – Taking Your Daughter to the Gents

When out, dads are often very embarrassed about taking their daughters to the loo but there may be emergency situations when they simply have to. The first hurdle is finding a toilet. A disabled toilet is generally the best option. If there isn't one available, you'll have to take her to the 'gents', in which case carry her straight into the cubicle to avoid her becoming curious and wandering off. Don't worry about the other men at the urinals – some will be dads and full of admiration, others will feel pity, and the majority won't even notice you.

Once inside the cubicle, give the seat a wipe with an antibacterial wipe (use toilet paper if you don't have wipes with you). Be quick because your little girl won't be able to hang on for long. Help your daughter on to the toilet (the disabled toilets are usually quite high up). Use a portable toilet seat if you have one, and offer to help hold your little girl on the toilet – she'll know what she wants.

When it comes to wiping, your daughter will probably be able to wipe herself after a wee, so just make sure she has a couple of sheets of toilet paper. Don't worry too much if she doesn't do a particularly good job – it's only wee. If she does a poo it's a different story as your daughter may still struggle with this. You'll need to wipe her from front to back to avoid infection. Make sure that you both wash your hands thoroughly afterwards.

THE NEXT FEW WEEKS

Once your daughter has become used to leaving home without her nappy, she's as good as potty trained. She'll become used to using public toilets when necessary, and to having a wee before leaving home. As she matures, she'll also find that she can 'hang on' for longer.

There will be occasional accidents – it's very common for three-year-olds to continue to have accidents every now and again – but you'll find that your daughter gradually becomes confident about taking herself off to the toilet unannounced at home, only asking for help with wiping after a poo. Accidents will become such a rarity that you'll soon start leaving the travel potty and eventually the change of clothes at home.

Encourage your little girl to use the toilet without her child's toilet seat because this will make going out much easier – you can always reintroduce the star chart as an extra incentive.

7

When Your Daughter Doesn't Fit the Mould

It's all very well giving a week-by-week guide to potty training your daughter, but little girls are all different and some simply won't comply. If this applies to your daughter, the following extra strategies will enable you to customise our potty-training method so that it works for her.

THE REBEL

Girls are naturally quite savvy and some will work out that accidents equal attention. Plenty of little girls have resorted to pooing and weeing for attention. This is particularly common when a new sibling arrives, leaving your daughter feeling very put out. It can also occur if there are other family stresses and your little girl isn't getting as much attention as she's used to.

Although it's shocking and disgusting to see your little princess deliberately pooing in her knickers like an angry convict, try to understand that she's still a baby herself and desperate for Mummy's love and attention. Your daughter is especially likely to 'protest' while you're breastfeeding the new baby because your attention will be instantly diverted from the baby to her – even if it is angry attention. As far as she's concerned, attention is attention and it makes no difference if it's angry attention.

Be reassured by the fact that protest pooing is normal and doesn't mean your daughter is deeply disturbed. It's easily dealt with by minimising your response. This is easier said than done, but do resist the temptation to freak out and yell because this will pretty much guarantee that your little girl repeats her performance. Pop your baby in his cot and clean your daughter up quickly and calmly without being chatty, using plenty of wipes and shoving dirty clothes in a bag to be dealt with later. Only start chatting and giving attention again to your little girl once you are settled back and feeding the baby.

Bear in mind that you were probably cooing over your newborn adoringly while your daughter watched unnoticed. Try giving your daughter a special dose of Mummy attention while you are breastfeeding by singing, telling stories or even watching children's television together. You could also try talking to her about her feelings – ask if she finds it difficult seeing you cuddling the baby because she wants a cuddle herself. Explain that babies take up a lot of time, but once the baby is asleep then you can have a lovely cuddle together. If she doesn't want to talk, just leave it. Your little girl will probably try protest pooing a few more times. Keep spare clothes and wipes to hand so that you can clean up really efficiently. If you keep your reaction consistent she'll soon give up.

Protest pooing can sometimes occur when parents are particularly 'nice' about cleaning up accidents. By all means give yourself a pat on the back for remaining calm when there's poo smeared around your home, but be careful that you don't inadvertently give your daughter a huge dose of kindly attention. We're not suggesting that you should get annoyed, but try to keep your response more neutral – aim to be calm and efficient rather than calm and kindly. When the mess is cleaned up, don't say much about it but switch to doing something completely different and only then give your little girl lots of chatty attention.

THE ENTHUSIAST

Some little girls are desperate to come out of nappies and wear pretty knickers like their older sister, cousins or friends. Although they are mentally ready, they are still very young and probably don't yet have the physical capabilities. The best way to deal with this is to give potty training a try to avoid this becoming a battle. Explain to your daughter that she can go without her nappy for a morning to see how she gets on. Do give her lots of praise for sitting on the potty, pulling her knickers up and down and so on, even if she proves incapable of knowing when she's about to wee or poo. After her session, give her lots of praise and tell her that she can have another go at using the potty another day – hopefully she'll forget about it for a little while before wanting another go.

In the meantime you could let her have her own 'knicker drawer' so the concept of growing up will still seem within her grasp. She'll probably enjoy taking her knickers out and admiring them, perhaps trying them on dolls.

THE ARTIST

If your daughter loves painting and colouring in, you may find that she becomes so absorbed in her drawings and has such excellent concentration that she sometimes wets herself. Becoming very involved in play is probably one of the most common reasons for girls to have accidents.

The problem will naturally resolve itself as the signals to go to the toilet become stronger with age, and also as her bladder develops, allowing her to 'hold on' for long enough to finish her picture. In the meantime you can suggest that your daughter goes to the toilet before her colouring, and don't make too much fuss when she has an accident. Just explain that she was concentrating so hard that her body didn't notice that it needed a wee – keep positive so that your little girl doesn't become self-conscious and worried about having accidents.

THE CHILD WHO DOESN'T MIND WET KNICKERS

Most little girls are fastidious about hygiene and won't stand for being in wet knickers. As a result, they will tell you the moment they have wet themselves and be eager to change into clean clothes. Because they don't like being wet they will be motivated to learn to use the potty quickly. Not all little girls are like this, however, and some really won't care about being wet.

If your daughter is quite laid back and happy to play for hours wearing wet knickers (a characteristic more often seen in little boys), do check her knickers and tights regularly to see if she's had an accident. She may end up a bit sore if she's wet for a long time. When you do discover that she's wet but hasn't told you, don't make a big deal about it. Just say, 'Oh, you've done a wee. Let's get you into nice fresh clothes.'

Don't give her extra attention – positive or negative. Remind yourself that she's not deliberately weeing in her knickers; she's still very young and simply learning. Okay, it may take her a little longer to learn than if she were more aware of being wet and soggy, but she'll get there before long and the day will come when she's dry all the time. In the meantime you can console yourself with the fact that she's not a fusspot.

THE CONTORTIONIST

Little girls with older brothers may insist on weeing standing up. If they push their tummies out, it's just about possible for girls to wee into the toilet while standing or against a tree, although it will probably be a bit messy. Watching your daughter standing to wee will seem a bit strange but she isn't weird, and it doesn't mean she'll grow up to be butch – she's just copying her brothers so don't make a big deal about it. You'll probably find that she grows out of it as soon as she starts nursery and sees other little girls weeing (at nursery, the toilet doors are usually very short and don't lock, and lots of children happily go to the toilet in full view of each other).

THE FALSE-ALARM CHILD

You've just got to the front of the queue at the bank and your little girl announces, 'Mummy, I need a poo.' Your obvious reply is, 'Can you wait a couple of minutes?' To which her obvious response is, 'No, it's coming now.' So you lose your place in the queue, curse as you realise you'll have to come back to the bank another time, then race off to find the nearest toilet. When you get there, your daughter sits down then calmly explains that she doesn't need to go any more.

Many parents would lose their temper at this point but that really isn't the answer. False alarms are quite common when children are toilet training, and your daughter may get genuinely confused from time to time about whether she needs the toilet or not. Also, the stress of rushing to find a toilet can sometimes stop her needing to go. If you react, this can easily become a great new device for getting your attention; or worse, it could make your daughter feel anxious about asking for the toilet next time. So bite your tongue, resist getting annoyed and simply say, 'Oh well. You can always try again later.' False alarms may go on for a few weeks and can be very tedious. Resist showing you're annoyed in any way and the problem will resolve itself.

THE LATE STARTER

Although lots of little girls have the physical ability to control their urine and bowel movements soon after their second birthday or earlier, there are plenty of exceptions. Don't push your daughter if she's a late starter because the pressure will make her feel anxious, especially when she clearly lacks the physical capability to progress. If you push her too soon, she'll probably fail and you'll have to restart potty training in a few months, dragging out the whole process.

Girls who are late starters are quite unusual as it tends to be boys who are the slow ones to come out of nappies. You're bound to know other little girls of her age or younger who are already potty trained. You have to do what is right for your daughter, though, and in this case it is to be patient and only proceed with potty training when she's showing the signs of being physically ready (*see Chapter 1*). There's also a chance that she's late to become mentally ready – again, unusual for girls but it happens. You must wait until she is showing the signs that she has the mental maturity before proceeding (*see Chapter 1*).

If your daughter is one of the slower ones to come out of nappies, it's important to abandon any preconceived ideas you may have had about getting her potty trained by a certain age. Instead, remind yourself that she will get there in the end. If she's six months behind her friends or cousins, so what? If you don't care, she certainly won't. In the meantime, you'll probably get a few comments and 'helpful suggestions' from well-meaning friends and relatives. Don't give in to their pressure. Be confident that you are doing what is right for your little girl – after all, you know her best. Explain to 'helpful' friends that your daughter isn't yet showing the signs that she's ready to come out of nappies; and when she is ready, you'll perhaps try out some of their suggestions. Grandmothers can be trickier because they are from a generation that tried to get children out of nappies as early as possible, driven by the fact that they may have used cloth nappies and possibly didn't have a washing machine. Reassure them that you are intending to start potty training your daughter within the next few months or so, but you are watching for signs that she has the physical capability. If all else fails and they keep going on, you could show them this book!

If your daughter ever starts asking why other girls wear knickers rather than nappies, simply use this as a cue to give potty training a go. If it turns out that she still isn't physically ready, see 'The Enthusiast' (*page 85*) for tips on persuading her to wait.

How to Resume Potty Training after a Failed Attempt

If your daughter has reached the age of three and is showing no willingness to use the potty, it's probably because you tried to train her before she was mature enough, or at a difficult time such as the arrival of a new baby, and she's come to associate potties with stress. She won't be the only one. You too will dread getting the potty out because you know it ends in accidents and tears.

You can resolve this. Although your daughter is old enough to be physically ready to come out of nappies, you need to help her to become mentally ready too because at the moment there's a bit of a block. Put her back in nappies for six weeks and don't mention potties or knickers unless your daughter does first.

After six weeks, ask your little girl if she'd like to have another go at using the potty. She will probably say no because she's testing you and making sure that the pressure really is off. So let her have her way and say,

'Okay, maybe another day.' Resist mentioning potties for another week then ask her again. Don't appear anxious or in any way bothered that she's not interested, and she'll probably agree after a couple more weeks. You can give her extra encouragement by showing her a packet of chocolate buttons and saying that she can earn these as well as stickers for every time she sits or does a wee on the potty. Although some parenting experts would frown about giving children sweets as 'bribes', plenty of mums will testify that it works. Once again, let your daughter be the one to decide whether today is the day.

When she finally agrees, she has effectively given her 'permission' to restart potty training so will be feeling in control and a lot less anxious than before. You will probably find that she learns very quickly. It's very unlikely that she won't ever agree because she'll be aware of other little girls her age using the potty or toilet and will eventually want to be like her peers.

8

Night Training

The first time your daughter goes to bed without wearing her nappy, you'll no doubt be bracing yourself to be woken in the small hours to change bedding and night clothes. Although bedwetting happens to pretty much all children from time to time, the upside is that girls generally have fewer problems with wetting the bed than boys and tend to go through the night earlier.

Girls often manage to stay dry at night around the time of their third birthday, a few months after they have been potty trained. Do remember, though, that all children are different and develop at varying rates. Some little girls will find it physically impossible to stay dry through the night until they are four or five. One in six five-year-olds regularly wets the bed, according to the Enuresis Resource and Information Centre. However, bedwetting is rarely anything to worry about (*see Chapter 9* to rule out any underlying medical problems). You can take comfort from the fact that health professionals don't even recognise bedwetting as a problem until the age of six because it is so common among small children. You only need to seek help from your doctor if, after the age of six, your daughter is wetting the bed more than twice a week.

As a parent, it's important to take a relaxed approach and to reassure your daughter so that she doesn't become anxious about wetting the bed or having to wear a nappy at night. It's particularly difficult for girls who are late night-time developers because they will be different to most other girls their age. Try not to worry that there's anything wrong with your daughter, or even that it is your fault in some way. You just have to accept that there's nothing you can do to speed things along because it's all down to your daughter's physical development, and this is controlled entirely by nature, not nurture.

HOW THE BODY DEVELOPS TO STAY DRY AT NIGHT

It's impossible for your little girl to have night control until she is physically mature enough. This is what must happen:

- She needs to produce enough vasopressin. This anti-diuretic hormone suppresses urination at night by slowing the production of urine. It tends to kick in from around 18 months, although in some children it doesn't do so until the age of six.

- Her nervous system must be mature enough. This will enable it to trigger a strong signal during sleep telling her that her bladder is full and needs emptying. This signal needs to be strong enough to wake her, so must be stronger than the full-bladder signals she receives during the day. This is why children usually learn to be toilet trained during the day before they can go without nappies at night.

- Her bladder needs to be large enough. This will mean it can hold a large enough quantity of urine to avoid needing to get up throughout the night. Bladders grow rapidly from the age of two until four, explaining why lots of children come out of night nappies once they are three.

WHEN TO LEAVE THE NIGHT NAPPY OFF

Most little girls will be ready to go without their night nappy a few months after they manage to be dry during the day – often around her third birthday and usually before the age of four. Girls generally find night control easier than boys, and some will learn to stay dry during the night at the same time as they come out of daytime nappies. Try leaving the night-time nappy off while potty training if you think your daughter is physically ready. More than three wet beds in a week suggest that she's not yet physically mature enough and should go back to night nappies.

Early Signs that She May Be Ready to Try

- She remains dry during her nap. This is one of the first indicators that your daughter has some control over her bladder during sleep. Once she is potty trained, put a fresh nappy on for her nap and see if it's still dry when she wakes up. You can start leaving her nap-nappy off once she has had 10 consecutive dry naps.

- She is able to 'hold on' for a wee. This shows good bladder control. As your daughter matures you'll notice that she is able to hang on longer before she wees. Once she can wait several minutes you could try leaving her nappy off at night if she's keen to give it a try.

- She says she doesn't want to wear a nappy at night. Lots of little girls are desperate to be grown-up and will decide themselves when they are ready to abandon their night nappy. You may well find that she is indeed ready to stay dry at night but some girls overestimate their maturity and will end up wetting the bed. Give it a couple of weeks and use nappy mats and towels to save on laundry. If, however, she's having more than three accidents a week, you could gently suggest that she waits a few more weeks for her body to be ready. If she's reluctant, then try getting her into pull-ups (*see page 107*).

Definite Signs that She is Ready to Try

- She wakes up in the night to wee in the toilet or potty. This shows she is well and truly ready to leave her night nappies behind. Her brain's signals that she needs a wee are now so strong that they wake her up. Be aware that most children don't get up for a wee in the night if they are wearing a nappy.

- Her nappies are still dry in the morning. This is a sure sign that she no longer needs to wear a nappy at night. She now has enough of the hormone vasopressin, which suppresses night-time urination. If she has had several consecutive dry morning nappies, let her have a nappy-free night. Note that some children will wee in their nappy as soon as they wake up and won't go to the toilet until they are not wearing a nappy.

When your daughter shows at least one of the above signs and only has very occasional accidents during the day, you can try leaving her nappy off at night.

HOW TO COME OUT OF NIGHT NAPPIES

Get her Permission

Ask if she'd like to try leaving off her night nappy, and go ahead only if she seems keen. If there is any reluctance on her part, simply postpone the big night for a couple of weeks or until your daughter is happy about the idea. It's important that she doesn't feel pushed into leaving off her night nappy because she'll get particularly anxious should she have an accident. Also, feeling stressed can sometimes make children more likely to wet the bed.

Buy a Big Bed and a Night Light

It's essential that your little girl is out of her cot and in a big bed before she starts night training or she won't be able to get to a potty or toilet during the night. You can leave a potty by the bed (not ideal if the bedroom is carpeted), or leave the potty in the upstairs toilet. Some little girls will happily use the toilet in the night, especially if they have become used to using the toilet, rather than the potty, during the day.

Make sure that there is either a night light in your daughter's bedroom or a hall light on so that your daughter can easily find her way to the toilet or potty in the night. If she does get up in the night for a wee, encourage her back to bed quickly. Don't give too much praise in the middle of the night or she'll become fully awake and may even want to play.

Protect the Bed

Use a mattress cover under the sheet – the plastic ones get a bit sweaty so we suggest you use a cotton-quilted one (available from most shops that sell bedding). You can give extra protection by putting a disposable nappy mat (from chemists) or a towel under your daughter's bottom in the early weeks. These can be whipped out in the middle of the night, usually leaving the bed dry underneath.

Monitor her Drinking Pattern

Ensure that your little girl has plenty to drink during the day because dehydration can irritate the bladder, making her want to wee more frequently. Once you're sure that she's getting plenty to drink, you can stop giving her drinks in the hour before bedtime. It may take a few days to adjust your daughter's drinking pattern.

Remind her to Have a Wee before Bedtime

Get into the habit of reminding your daughter to have a wee before she goes to bed. If she's been in bed a while before lights out, ask if she needs a wee before going to sleep. Offer to help her get out of bed because she may be feeling too tired to bother otherwise.

Wake her for a Night Wee

Your daughter may sleep for up to 12 hours at night, which is a long time for anyone to go without having a wee. It may be worth getting her up for a wee during the first couple of months of night training to reduce her chances of wetting the bed. Make sure that you wake her up and that she doesn't 'wee in her sleep', which will lead to bad habits and make bedwetting more likely.

When you wake her, usually before you go to bed yourself, you may find that she takes ages to actually have a wee and sometimes doesn't seem to need one. Once you've helped her on to the potty or toilet, ask if she needs a wee – she may only be able to nod or shake her head as she'll be too tired to speak. Also, try turning on a tap as the sound of running water may help her to wee. You'll find that after a few nights she gets used to being woken up for a wee and will be able to perform a bit quicker. There will be occasions when she simply doesn't need to go, so do accept this and pop her back to bed even if she hasn't been. There's still a reasonable chance she'll stay dry until morning.

What to Do when She Wets the Bed

It's not a matter of *if* she wets the bed but *when*. Just about all children will wet the bed when they are learning to go through the night. This means having to wake up and change bed linen. Stay calm and never show any signs of irritation with your daughter. Keep a spare nightdress and sheet to hand so that you can sort your daughter out quickly. If you've put a towel or nappy mat down, you may find that the sheet is still dry underneath, which makes things very easy.

The Next Morning

Make a big fuss of your daughter if she managed to remain dry. If she did wet the bed, don't worry or get cross – it wasn't your daughter's fault and shows that she's not physically mature enough to stay dry every night. Never assume it was because she was too lazy to get out of bed to wee. Be patient, and kindly explain to your little girl that our bodies grow up at different rates and that hers is still changing so that one day she will find it easy not to wet the bed.

Should You Continue?

When your little girl starts night training, do bear in mind that a few accidents are completely normal and to be expected. However, if she's having more than three accidents in a week, then her body probably isn't yet mature enough so put her back in nappies for a month or two. If she's staying dry most nights and only having one or two accidents a week persevere because in a couple more weeks she'll have even fewer wet nights. Should she get very upset by the accidents, you can always pop her back in night nappies to allow her time to mature a little more.

TROUBLESHOOTING

She Refuses to Wear a Nappy at Night

Lots of little girls are keen to be 'big girls' and will make a fuss about wearing a nappy at night even if they keep wetting the bed. Try persuading your daughter that pull-ups are 'big girl night nappies', or let her decorate a pull-up nappy with felt-tip pens and stickers during the day and call it 'princess night knickers'. Tell her she's only allowed to wear it at night, and come bedtime she will hopefully be keen to put it on.

It Seems Impossible for her to Learn to Stay Dry at Night

Plenty of little girls still need night nappies when they are four and may wet the bed occasionally even when they are five. Some will remain in night nappies until they are six. If your daughter is a late developer it's essential never to pressurise her but accept that her body simply isn't mature enough for her to stay dry at night. Just give her masses of reassurance and talk to her about bladder size and brain signals. Explain that once her body is ready she will find it easy to stay dry every night.

She's Been Invited to a Sleepover but She still Wets the Bed

Being a late developer is particularly hard for girls as they are more socially mature than boys and many start to have sleepovers from about the age of four or five. Sadly, there's no magic way to make her stay dry at night when she stays with friends, and she'll actually be more likely to wet the bed if she's anxious.

When she gets the sleepover invite, do ask her if she actually wants to go – she may decide that she doesn't because of the risk of wetting the bed. If she does want to go then mention her bedwetting to the other child's mother, and tell your daughter that she can tell the other mum if she does wet the bed.

We suggest buying night pants, which are pull-up nappies in pretty designs shaped to look more like knickers than a nappy. Available from chemists, they are disposable and your daughter could wear one under her nightdress. You can also buy incontinence briefs online. These don't look as nappy-like as the disposables and are basically briefs with a sewn-in absorbent pad. They are available in tiny sizes, from two to three years and upwards.

Just like potty training, night training can't be rushed. When it happens will be very much dictated by your daughter's physical development and all you can do in the meantime is gently guide her and be very patient.

9

Resolving Common Medical Problems

When children have trouble with potty training or bedwetting, you just have to wait patiently for them to mature and the problem will usually resolve itself. Occasionally, however, there is a medical condition at the root of your child's training troubles. If this is the case then you'll need to see your doctor. Here are some conditions to be aware of.

URINARY TRACT INFECTION (UTI)

This is 10 times more common among girls than boys because they have a much shorter urethra (tube that leads from the bladder to outside the body), which makes it easier for bacteria to enter the body. If your daughter suddenly starts to wet herself after being dry for a while, or she wets the bed more often, it may be due to an infection. This is because urinary tract infections cause more frequent weeing. Other symptoms to look out for include: doing a small amount of wee at a time; pain on urination; fishy-smelling urine; a fever; vomiting; and abdominal pain.

What You Can Do

Although anxiety can be the reason for bedwetting or more frequent accidents you should take your little girl to the doctor in case she has an infection. A simple urine test will show if there is an infection that needs to be treated with antibiotics. To help prevent re-infection, and to help stop your daughter getting a urinary tract infection in the first place, always wipe her from front to back. This reduces the chances of bacteria from the anus entering the vagina. Also, give her plenty to drink because a faster and more frequent flow of urine gives bacteria less time to multiply in the bladder.

VULVOVAGINITIS

Lots of little girls suffer from this when they come out of nappies. Gut bacteria (found in poo) are transferred from the anal region to the vagina and vulva, causing inflammation, soreness and itchiness. It's therefore important that little girls have help wiping thoroughly and from front to back.

Although baby girls can get covered in poo, they generally don't get vulvovaginitis because their nappies are changed quickly. Once out of nappies, though, if a little girl does a bad job of wiping herself after a poo she could remain a bit 'dirty' for hours on end until she has a bath or someone checks and wipes her properly – perhaps when she gets home from nursery or school. Also, once little girls are out of nappies they can scratch themselves, making the skin around the vagina and vulva more vulnerable to infection – and of course touching herself can transfer infection.

Vulvovaginitis isn't serious and doesn't affect girls after the age of about eight as the body prepares for puberty and starts to make oestrogen, which strengthens the vaginal skin.

What You Can Do

Your doctor may take a swab and prescribe antibiotics, antibacterial cream or oestrogen cream to help minimise any discomfort. You can take steps to try to avoid the condition in the first place and to manage it if your daughter does suffer because it can be quite uncomfortable. Whenever possible, then, help your daughter to wipe herself – especially after a poo – and always from front to back. If she's fiercely independent, let her have the first couple of wipes then say something like, 'You've done so well I bet Mummy can't wipe any more off.' Cotton knickers and avoiding bubble bath can also help reduce irritation, and do keep your daughter's nails short to minimise scratching the skin.

THRUSH

This is a fungal infection caused by *Candida albicans*, which thrives in warm damp conditions such as the vagina. As well as being sore and itchy, there is a thick white discharge. Thrush isn't a sexually transmitted disease – it's a common infection that can affect people of all ages. It's often seen after antibiotics for another condition such as tonsillitis or an ear infection.

What You Can Do

If you suspect your daughter may have thrush, seek medical help because this fungal infection is easily treated. Your doctor will probably prescribe an anti-fungal cream and you should see an improvement within a couple of days. It's important to continue the treatment after symptoms have disappeared to prevent a recurrence. Again, cotton knickers can help because the cooler your daughter is, the less prone she will be to infection.

DIABETES

Every year, more than 1,500 children in Britain develop diabetes mellitus – the amount of sugar in the blood is too high and the excess glucose is passed out of the body in the urine. If your daughter has diabetes, she will wee a lot more and be very thirsty, even getting up in the night for a drink. She may also seem generally lethargic and unwell, and sometimes children with diabetes will suddenly start having more accidents and wetting the bed.

What You Can Do

Get medical help because diabetes must be managed with insulin injections. You will also be told how to help balance your daughter's blood sugar levels by ensuring that she eats regularly and sticks to particular foods.

CONSTIPATION

Dry, hard poos and straining on the toilet are sure signs of constipation. Address this quickly because constipation can become painful and your daughter may start to withhold her poos and make the problem worse. It may even cause anal fissures (*see page 118*).

If you don't sort this condition out, your daughter could develop chronic constipation and overflow incontinence. This is when dry, hard stools become lodged in the back passage and any poo that manages to get past gets squashed, broken up and looks like diarrhoea. You may notice that her knickers are smeared with poo even if you're sure that her bottom is being wiped properly. Eventually, your daughter will start soiling her pants because the poo that is lodged in the rectum confuses the sensations in the bowel and she won't know when her bowel is full and she needs a poo. The final stage of chronic constipation is that she will become unable to tell when she needs a wee and start wetting herself.

What You Can Do

- See your doctor who will confirm constipation by feeling your daughter's tummy, and rule out any rare anatomical problems. Sometimes an X-ray is arranged to confirm this. Your doctor may prescribe laxatives and stool softeners.

- Stress can make constipation worse, so reassure your daughter that it's not her fault if she's been pooing in her knickers.

- Make sure that your daughter drinks plenty because dehydration can slow bowel movements.

- Gradually introduce more fibre into her diet by giving her more fruit, vegetables, dried fruit, beans, porridge and brown bread. It's important to increase her fibre intake very gradually because a sudden, large increase will probably cause wind, bloating, tummy ache and diarrhoea.

- If your daughter's poos have been dry, hard and painful she may have become anxious about going to the toilet. Make sure, though, that she doesn't hold on when she needs to go because poos can change from soft to hard in a few hours. Get her to the toilet quickly when she says she needs a poo and encourage her to go by reassuring her that pooing won't be so painful if she goes now rather than later, and if she drinks plenty and eats the fibrous food you give her. Explaining to your daughter what constipation is and how you are sorting it out will help her to feel less anxious.

ANAL FISSURE

A small tear in the anus can cause very painful pooing and also some bleeding (the bleeding is nothing to worry about once a fissure has been diagnosed). The cause of fissures is usually constipation – forcing out hard stools (*see page 116*). Your daughter will be reluctant to poo, particularly in the potty or toilet if she's only recently started potty training. If she's in pain, she'll opt instead for the familiarity of her nappy.

Straining can also cause anal fissures. A bit of pushing is fine but if your daughter is really struggling then suggest that she tries to do a poo a bit later instead (usually another five minutes or so). Straining can be a sign that she's a bit constipated so do watch her diet and fluid intake.

What You Can Do

See your GP because it's important to get a diagnosis, particularly if you spot any bleeding. Your GP may prescribe a soothing cream to put on your daughter's perianal region (the area around the anus). Healing can take a while because the skin in the anus is wet. A small dab of Vaseline to lubricate the anus just before your daughter does a poo can help alleviate discomfort.

Because anal fissures nearly always result from constipation it's essential to get this sorted out. Do follow all the tips on avoiding constipation (*above*) as this condition can make anal fissures particularly painful. The fissure won't be able to heal if your daughter remains constipated.

ADHD, AUTISM AND OTHER LEARNING DIFFICULTIES

L earning difficulties make potty training particularly challenging, and if your daughter is affected you'll need masses of patience. Don't attempt to get her out of nappies too soon because having a 'false start' would be very disruptive for her. You want to be sure that she is physically ready.

What You Can Do

Follow our method. This should work well as it aims to minimise the pressure put on the child. Be prepared for potty training to take longer than it takes other children. Ask your doctor or whoever helps you with your daughter's condition about getting some help with potty training. They may also give you some advice and tips that are relevant to teaching your daughter.

Frustrating Days

If your daughter's toilet training is delayed because of a medical condition then do be reassured that there is plenty of help available. On those frustrating days when you think she'll never succeed, just remind yourself that she will get there in the end – and what's a few extra months anyway?

10

Moving Forwards

and will learn more confidence about being away from you.

ACCIDENTS AND SETBACKS

When accidents are a rare occurrence and your daughter is confident about going to the toilet, we'd say that she was potty trained. Although this happens relatively painlessly for most little girls, some will take a while to reach this stage. If your daughter is one of the slower ones, it will sometimes feel as though she'll never be reliably dry, but she will get there – probably without you even noticing. You'll suddenly realise one day that your daughter hasn't wet herself for a while.

Whether your daughter was quick or slow to come out of nappies, over the coming weeks and months you'll see her becoming more independent – taking herself off to the toilet without even asking, and needing less and less help with wiping and hand washing. Her new skills will give her lots of confidence, and you and your daughter will feel proud as she makes this momentous step away from her baby years towards becoming a little girl. When she goes on play dates and starts school and nursery she'll be at a big advantage and will feel more confident about being away from you because she is fully toilet trained.

ACCIDENTS AND SETBACKS

Diarrhoea

Diarrhoea is common among toddlers, and if your daughter picks up an infection she is likely to soil her knickers. This doesn't mean that she's regressed; she's simply unwell. We suggest that you put her back in nappies for a day or so to save on mess. Be sensitive to your daughter and explain that a nappy would just be worn while she's ill and needs to rush to the toilet. Tell her it's difficult to get to the toilet in time, even for adults. If she's very reluctant to wear a nappy then don't force her – she's unlikely to have diarrhoea for more than about 24 hours.

Wetting the Bed

If your daughter is dry during the day but still wets the bed or even needs nappies at night, she is still, by our definition, 'potty trained'. Staying dry at night relies on your daughter being physically mature enough, which is all down to nature, so we always say that nights don't count.

Dealing with Accidents

Once your daughter has been dry for a while, don't worry if she suddenly has an accident. Most children wet themselves between the ages of three and four, and sometimes will even poo in their pants. Although common, it generally happens only a couple of times a month so your daughter is still 'potty trained'. Once again, it's simply a waiting game for parents as your daughter matures and slowly stops having any accidents at all.

When she does have an accident, she may feel as though she has failed because she will have come to associate using the toilet with lots of praise. Make light of it so that her confidence isn't knocked. Tell her that even big girls have accidents sometimes, and perhaps say, 'Never mind, these things happen. You must have been too busy concentrating on your colouring to remember to go to the toilet.'

Dealing with Setbacks

Sometimes your little girl will have more than just a random accident and will start wetting herself frequently, despite having been dry for months. Setbacks generally occur when she is stressed and can happen around the time of starting nursery, the arrival of a new sibling or perhaps moving house. Your daughter may start wetting herself in the run-up to these stressful events or once they have occurred. The best way to deal with a setback is not to deal with it. Make light of any accidents. Remember that accidents can also be a way of getting attention, which is another reason not to make too much fuss.

Some little girls will want to start using their potty again or even to wear a nappy. If this happens with your daughter, let her. She's only trying to be the much-loved baby so give her plenty of fuss and attention. She'll soon get fed up with soggy nappies and messy potties. Setbacks don't generally go on for more than a few weeks so keep your response to your little girl's regression low key and wait for it to pass.

We hope that you and your daughter have enjoyed our relaxed approach to potty training. We would like to leave you with some checkpoints to assess your daughter's progress.

Ten Signs that Your Daughter is Fully Potty Trained

1. You no longer even think about packing spare knickers and tights for her when you go out.

2. If she doesn't do a wee before she leaves home it's not a problem – you won't be searching for a toilet within the next 10 minutes.

3. Her pretty knickers are starting to look old and worn out.

4. The potty has become dusty and forgotten because she uses the toilet.

5. If you're going away for the night, you only pack one nightdress for her and don't bother taking a spare.

6. When you visit your local café you no longer glance over at the toilet to check there isn't an 'out of order' sign or a long queue.

7. When you go somewhere new you don't do an automatic check to see where the toilets are the minute you arrive.

8. She knows how to wipe from front to back and can wash her hands by herself.

9. You don't have to plan toilet stops on long car journeys – she goes when everyone else goes and there's never a wet car seat.

10. At home, your daughter trots off to the toilet by herself without even telling you.

Ticking three or more of these points shows that your daughter is well and truly toilet trained, so well done. If you can't tick the above points then your daughter isn't there yet so do keep up the encouragement and praise, and be patient. It will happen, we promise. In a couple of months or so, nappies and potties will start to become a distant memory, and when you hear other mums earnestly discussing the perils of toilet training, you'll wonder what on earth all the fuss is about.

Index

Also available from Vermilion

Potty Training Boys
. . . the easy way

You're not alone in feeling slightly nervous about starting to potty train your son. Questions such as 'How will I know when he's ready?' and 'How do I begin?' are common to many parents.

This simple, reassuring guide is packed with all the information you need, including what to do on the first day; tips on specific 'boy' problems; what to do if your son refuses to sit on the potty or is a late starter; and how to fit potty training into your schedule.

9780091917340   £5.99